Using Data to Build Better Products

A Hands-On Guide to Working with Data in R&D - The Basics

JAN BOSCH

ISBN: 1541210808
ISBN-13: 978-1541210806

PREFACE

We live in a data-centric world where everything we do and the way our products behave can and often is recorded. It's easy to lament about the potential negative implications for privacy and anonymity, but that really would miss the great benefits provided by data: unprecedented quality of user experience and product performance as companies use the, typically anonymized, data for significantly improved decision making in R&D and elsewhere.

Despite the promise of big data, the fact of the matter is that companies collect extensive amounts of data but fail to make use of the data sitting in the data warehouses, lakes and oceans. Even the most advanced companies that we work with admit to 99% of their data being black, meaning that there is no understanding of the content and meaning of that data, while up to 1% is considered dark, dark grey, meaning that there is some insight derived from the data.

Research by us and others shows that more than half of the features developed in R&D do not deliver on the value expected at the time of feature prioritization. In addition, we see that companies spend vast amounts of R&D resources, frequently north of 80%, in commodity functions of their products, rather than on innovative and differentiating features. Adopting data-driven and evidence-based decision making can provide a powerful antidote for these ways of investing in and performing R&D.

When we published the Speed, Data and Ecosystems book [3] there were several requests for a shorter, easy to read and illustrated introduction to working with data in product development. This short book is the response to those demands from the market. It provides a detailed, hands-on and story-driven approach to working with data in product development. It describes the typical steps that companies go through as they build their capability, starting from understanding product use to experimenting with features to, finally, value modeling of features and tracking the delivery of this feature during iterative development.

We hope you enjoy reading the short book and manage to apply these principles in your R&D organization and day to day work. This book holds the promise of doubling the effectiveness of your R&D. Make sure to capitalize on that promise!

CONTENTS

ACKNOWLEDGMENTS

Books are never written in isolation and this book is no exception. The ideas presented in this book are the result of collaborations with and learnings from a great many people and companies. For the last five years, I have had the privilege of leading the Software Center, a collaboration between, today, 10 companies (Ericsson, Volvo Cars, AB Volvo, Saab Defense, Siemens, Grundfos, Jeppesen (part of Boeing), Axis Communications (part of Canon), Tetra Pak and Verisure) and five universities (Chalmers University of Technology, Gothenburg University, Malmö University, Linköping University and Mälardalen University. Before Software Center, I have had the opportunity to work for Intuit when data-driven development and experimentation were actively being adopted. Also, over the years, I have done work with and visited great European and international companies such as Booking, Spotify, Klarna, King, Rovio and Microsoft.

In my research, I have had the opportunity to work with many talented researchers, but some require explicit mention. Helena Holmström Olsson and I have worked on the data-driven development topic for years now and we have built a wonderful and productive partnership with numerous publications. Three years ago we were joined by Aleksander Fabijan as a PhD student and his work has been a wonderful complement to the topics that Helena and I work on.

Finally, Petra, my life partner, is also a researcher that I collaborate and publish with on a regular basis. Some of the more management oriented work that we have done together forms part of the foundation of the ideas presented here.

Although the ideas presented here are the result of collaboration with others, the final responsibility for this short book lies with me and any omissions, mistakes and errors are mine.

1 INTRODUCTION

In almost every conscious moment of our lives, we take decisions. At home, we decide what to wear, what to eat, what to watch on television, who to connect with, etc. At work, we decide what products to build, what features to add to products, what customers to focus on, whether to fix a bug or build a workaround, whether to go to that meeting or to look for a way to skip it, etc. Most of the decisions we make, we make often. And lazy and resource optimising as we are, decisions we make often easily turn into routines and habits. Although it's efficient to make decisions without having to think about them (even if one can claim it's not a decision at all), the danger is that the decision we make is far from the optimal one.

Organisations have similar decision processes where decisions are automated in processes and tools, become hammer items during meetings or are driven by a set of norms, beliefs and values that make the outcome of a decision process virtually unavoidable. Whereas we can change our way of decision making with a bit of conscious effort when it is clear that the outcome of the decision is not the desired one, organisations have a much harder time to incorporate these kinds of changes. Once the "path" to reach a specific decision has been drawn in the organisation's "brain", it becomes increasingly difficult to change it. There are many contributing factors, but a primary one is that to change anything, in most organisations everyone involved in the activity needs to agree and one dissenting voice can block the entire change. Consequently, as they age, organisations, just like humans, become more and more set in their ways.

At the dawn of the age of enlightenment, we stopped blindly accepting truths claimed by authority figures and religion. Instead, we demanded evidence before accepting theories, models and claims. The adoption of the Scientific Method lead to an explosion of societal progress unimaginable by earlier generations. Although there is a fair share of "apocaholics" (people addicted to predicting the next apocalypse) among us, it is hard to argue against the fact that we have the best lives of any generation of humans in the history of time.

The fact remains, however, that we tend to use the scientific method and data-driven decision making to only a small slice of our lives. One of the reasons for not applying it everywhere is cost — intellectual, temporal, financial, etc. It is costly to define the hypothesis, experiment, collect the data and draw conclusions.

With the advent of "Big Data" however, we are able to decrease the cost of data-driven decision making with one or more orders of magnitude. It is now feasible to apply the Scientific Method to many more areas of our private lives (for instance the quantified self movement, Google Scholar, Klout.com, etc.). It is especially in our professional lives where data-driven decision making can now be applied to a much greater extent. During product development, in organisations and even while governing the ecosystems in which we operate, using data to make better decisions is not only possible but required to maintain our competitiveness.

This book is concerned with the transition from habitual, opinion based decision making to evidence-based decision making in all parts of our professional lives. In our collaboration with numerous companies, we've learned that the use of data is not something that we can limit to one aspect of our professional lives, but rather is something that, over time, starts to infuse all aspects of decision making.

2 WORKING WITH DATA

Humans work with the data in a typical process, consisting of four activities. These are collect, analyse, visualise and decide. First, the data needs to be *collected*. Typically this requires instrumenting software so that events are recorded and sent for storage.

Second, the data needs to be *analysed*. The analysis can be conducted manually or it can be supported by various tools. Companies that use dashboards tend to automate the analysis of the data to prepare for the next activity.

Visualisation is the third element of the human data loop. Here data is presented in such a way that humans can interpret the analysis of the data in meaningful ways. The focus is on highlighting that which is relevant, different or otherwise noteworthy.

Finally, the data is used for *decision making*. Although humans have great intuitions, we tend to make better decisions when we have clearly presented data available.

We explicitly talk about the human data loop as there are increasingly many techniques available where machines use data to make decisions and adjust their behaviour based on data. These systems operate in a data-driven fashion without human involvement and this is often referred to as "autonomous systems". We believe that human and automated data-driven decision making needs to be combined in a uniform framework, but that is the topic of an upcoming book.

3 INTRODUCING QUAME

After all this theoretical stuff, let's move on and introduce QuaMe, the imaginary case that we use throughout this book to illustrate and exemplify the concepts that we present. QuaMe is a startup in the wearables space and its aim is to serve the quantified self movement with cool products. For those that are unaware of the quantified self community: these are people that seek to collect in depth qualitative data about their life through the use of technology. Members of the quantified self movement, similar to us, want to take better decisions about their life using quantified data.

QuaMe (of course an abbreviation of "quantify me") has been going for a year and their first product is a bracelet called QMB (Quantify Me Better) – seen in the picture below. QMB can measure all kinds of cool things, ranging from stress levels and sleep patterns to blood sugar and heart rate. Their user community loves the QuaMe device and the company has the first couple of thousands rabidly enthusiastic users religiously tracking their stats.

QMB is a great looking piece of mechanics and hardware, but its core is the software. The software allows the price of the device to be so low as it manages to get accurate data out of very cheap sensors. The bracelet is connected to the internet through a cellular connection and, where available, Wi-Fi and connects to your phone using Bluetooth. Of course, there is a mobile companion app and users also get a cloud service associated with the device to store and track their data, analyse trends and summarise averages.

QMB is marketed as a "smart device" and the promise is that "your bracelet gets better every day you use it". The approach to accomplishing this is a combination of smart customisation by the device itself and continuous deployment of software whenever new versions are available.

The company was founded by Frida and Sven. Frida is a skilled software developer with basic knowledge of hardware and mechanics whereas Sven is a product manager and designer with some experience in ethnography. Both love math and numbers, even if they haven't used their university math skills much in their previous jobs. However, they often discuss the experiments that some of their friends in Web 2.0 companies run with their customers, such as A/B experiments, and how the data from these experiments allows these companies to make much more informed decisions.

As QuaMe is a company, they need to generate revenue. There are two main sources of income. The first is device sales where QMB is generating the first, upfront revenue that each customer provides. The second source is the sales of services on top of the basic functionality of the device. Thanks to earlier research and some very forgiving early users, the company is able to offer a variety of services including tracking sleep, stress, heart rate, blood sugar as well as, of course, location. Because of this,

QuaMe also offers support for different types of sports, including performance and calorie usage. Now they are expanding into movement analysis and other advanced sports coaching functionality. Finally, with the emergence of the internet of things (IoT), the company is exploring how QMB can play a role in this industry.

4 UNDERSTANDING PRODUCT USE

Although product companies typically add new features to extend the functionality of their products, the same companies have very little understanding of the use of these features. This means that companies invest major R&D resources with little insight into the effectiveness of these investments. As there is research that shows that for most companies more than half the features in a typical system are hardly ever or never used. This means that in a typical company, half of the R&D investments are wasted. In fact, it is even worse as the unused features complicate the system, causing cluttering of the user interface and dead code in the system that increases cost of maintenance and potentially affecting performance, reliability and other quality attributes.

With the emergence of big data thinking in industry, product managers, architects and engineers have turned their attention towards the effectiveness of R&D investments and to use data to generate insight product performance and customer usage patterns. The process of gaining insight follows the human data loop introduced earlier. For understanding product use, there are four steps:

- **Instrument code**: In order to measure actual customer or product behaviour, the events representing these behaviours need to be recorded. Typically this requires instrumentation of the code that can then be used to create streams of event data.

- **Collect data:** Once the code has been instrumented and the software deployed, the events are generated by the systems. Most companies decide to centralise the storage of event data through a cloud service.

- **Analyse data**: The raw event data will need to be processed to provide the insights that are needed. Typically, this involves identifying patterns in the data and detecting the incidence of these patterns in the data.

- **Visualising and decision making**: Finally, the results of the data analysis need to be presented and used for decision making. In many cases, presentation of results triggers new questions that drive the next iteration of the human data loop.

5 HOW THE QMB IS USED

At QuaMe, the company is a case study in conflicting emotions. On the one hand, QMB is selling well and the first 1000 bracelets are in the hands of customers. The reviews from bloggers and magazines in the quantified self movement are very positive. On the other hand, Frida and Sven have never worked so hard in their lives. They managed to build strong relationships with their suppliers and a set of contractors helping them out on various tasks. However, in the end, they are at the core of the network and almost all decisions flow through them. The more important concern is that they know that this initial surge of positive energy around QMB will not last. The product is in the honeymoon period as everyone likes something new and different. Everyone is in the "wow" phase. It is the role of Frida and especially Sven, as product manager, to build an easy transition for users to enter the "flow" phase. In the "flow" phase, users will use the bracelet continuously and integrate it into their lives and set habits.

Instrument code	Collect data	Analyse data	Visualising and decision making

As QuaMe wants to offer a user experience that integrates the use of QMB into their users' lives, the first step is to understand what functionality is the most important for the users. Frida and Sven have been so busy building the basic product that they haven't spent any time thinking about the instrumentation of their product for data collection. There is some data collected in each device, but these mostly are logs related to product quality. Also, these logs are not always sent back to QuaMe and, if collected, often sent in batches. The good news is, however, that the product software is explicitly designed to be continuously deployed so that Frida and Sven don't have to wait forever to start collecting data. Also, a bit of analysis shows that sending data on product use back to the company will be no problem as the bracelet already sends back data related to the customer. The product use data constitutes only a fraction of the overall data budget and hence it will not be a problem from a cost perspective.

QMB has a small colour display and a button that allows the user to rotate through a sequence of views. The current views include time, calories burned today, stress level, heart rate and sugar level. There are some other measurements that the bracelet performs, but these are accessed through the mobile phone app and cloud service. Sven and Frida decide to start with measuring the relative time each function is present on the screen of the bracelet.

INSTRUMENTING THE CODE

The very first step in any data initiative is to ensure that the data that you need is actually being generated. Really, the very first thing in most companies is to check if the data is already available, somewhere in the business, but with QuaMe being a young startup, we can skip over this step. The next step is to decide what data to collect and how to instrument the code such that we can collect it. In this case, our goal is to measure what the relative frequency of use is for each of the views provided by QMB. This requires a way of generating data and Frida and Sven decide that they will create an event record every time the view on the screen is changed. When creating event records, the next question becomes what data to collect. We want to collect enough to ensure we can capture all relevant information, but also minimise the amount of data that needs to be processed, communicated and stored.

Really, the very first thing in most companies is to check if the data is ALREADY available, somewhere in the business.

For a basic event record, we need at least the following elements:

- **Device or User Identity**: For a variety of reasons, including privacy laws, QuaMe uses device identity rather than user identity. Of course, with some analysis, the two can be easily correlated as users register their device with the company, but in this way user information is more contained.

- **Timestamp**: For any event, one needs to know when it happened. Otherwise, conducting analysis on the event data is highly complicated. The question then becomes what the resolution of the timestamp should be. As QMB runs a scaled down version of Linux, the resolution could be very high, but for practical reasons there is no added value. Just to be on the safe side, Frida decides that timestamps will have a resolution of 0.1 seconds.

- **Event ID**: The event ID can be designed such that each unique type of event is an ID or such that similar types of events share an ID and there is an additional data item making the event unique. For QMB, this means that we could have an event ID for each view (e.g., #1101 for time, #1102 for calories burned, etc.) or a combination of event ID and argument, e.g., #11 for view change and #01 for time, #02 for calories, etc. For QMB, Frida and Sven decide to take the first approach.

The length of the event record, with this is 10 bytes where 4 bytes are allocated to device identity, 4 bytes to the timestamp and 2 bytes to the event ID. In Table 1, the event types are shown. Each event is generated at the moment the view is activated in the device.

Table 1. Event types and corresponding event IDs.

Event type	TimeView	CalorieView	StressView	HeartRateView	SugarView
Event ID	#1101	#1102	#1103	#1104	#1105

COLLECTING DATA

Once we know the structure of the event record and we have decided where to insert the code in the system to generate the event record, the next decision we need to make is the *balance of computation* on the device itself versus the computation in the cloud as well as the *frequency of data uploading*. On the one hand, we could ask the device to perform all analysis and send the summary to the server. On the other hand, we could send each event record to the server. The advantage of doing the former is that it decreases the amount of data communicated between the device and the server whereas the advantage of the latter is that it allows for more types of analysis that can be conducted on historical data once it becomes available.

The frequency of uploading data to the server also needs to be considered. The device can either send each event as soon as it becomes available or it stores several events and then sends these out as a batch to the server. In the case of QMB, Frida and Sven decide to send all events to the server as the device has limited computational power and battery life is already a concern. However, to minimise the cost of communication, they decide to batch the data until the device is using a Wi-Fi connection.

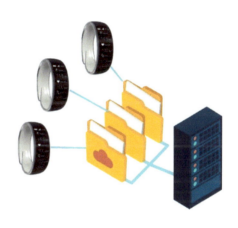

With all the decisions in place, Frida spends a couple of days coding the solution into the device software. When the function associated with a button press is called, the device now generates an event record that is put in a queue. A separate process periodically checks on the presence of a Wi-Fi connection and, if present, sends the contents of the queue to the server. Once the device software is completed and tested, Frida spends another day setting up the server to collect usage data. As QMB already has a cloud solution associated with it and all kinds of data relevant for customers is already stored there, Frida decides that just adding another table on that server will be the easiest solution in the short term.

Once everything is in place and verified, the software enters the release process. QuaMe uses an iterative release process where the software first goes out to a small set of customers that have agreed to test early releases. If no issues are reported the software is released in a number of waves to more and more devices until all devices have the latest release of the software.

Immediately after the software is deployed at the first devices, the data from them starts to flow in. Initially, the number of events per minute is only a handful, but with thousands of devices out there, the number goes up as number of QMBs getting the new software developed goes up and these start generating the data. Frida decided to store the events in MongoDB, a database that she has worked with in the past. Although it's not clear that this will work when the number of devices and types of events goes up some orders of magnitude, for now it works fine. As it's fine that the database loses some small number of events, the write process is set up as asynchronous which allows for faster write operations.

As an example of part of the event record, Table 2 shows some event records. As the table shows, the event records are stored as a sequence of records. Each record contains device ID, timestamp and event ID. This basic table is used for data analysis in the next section.

Table 2. Sample data of event records.

Device ID	Timestamp	Event ID
0.000.001.1070	2016-11-05 07:43:01:5	#1101
0.000.001.2154	2016-11-05 07:44:53:2	#1104
0.000.001.1521	2016-11-05 07:46:11:9	#1105
0.000.001.3009	2016-11-05 07:49:21:1	#1102
0.000.001.1070	2016-11-05 07:50:23:4	#1102

DATA ANALYSIS

As the database is starting contain thousands of events, Frida generates some scripts to analyse the data. As the initial intent was to learn about the relative frequency of use of the different views, she writes script that is automatically started some time after midnight to go through the list of device IDs and for each device ID calculate the duration of each view until it transitions. Then it calculates the average length of each view for each device ID during the last day. Once it has completed this calculation for each device ID, it calculates averages for each view over all the devices.

As the company has a screen set up in the office to show relevant information, Frida decided to add a dashboard view to it where she shows the daily average for each view, complemented with weekly and monthly averages.

To illustrate some of the calculation, in Table 2 device ID 0.000.001.1070 is present twice. Frida's script calculates the difference between the first and the second timestamps which is 04:20:4, or four minutes, twenty and four-tenth seconds. As the first event is #1101, this means that the time view was used for that amount of time. Calculating this for each device ID, this means that for a day the views should add up to 24 hours. In the Table 3, the average for November 5th is shown for device ID 0.000.001.1070. As you can see from the table, the time view is used far more than any other view on the bracelet.

Table 3. Average view duration for one device.

View	Duration
TimeView	18:25
CalorieView	03:35
StressView	00:06
HeartRateView	01:50
SugarView	00:04

VISUALIZING AND DECISION MAKING

It took a few days, due to their hectic schedules, but finally Frida had a chance to share her findings with Sven. When they saw the numbers, new questions surfaced in addition to the basic one concerned with the relative use of the different views. This was caused by the gap between what they had expected to see and what the data actually showed. During their analysis, there were two primary insights that they gained.

First, the time view was used much more than what either of them had expected. As the QMB bracelet primarily serves the quantified self movement, the notion of the bracelet just being used as a watch is a surprising and a bit unexpected use of the functionality. With just very basic watch functionality, they are even more surprised that this view is used so frequently.

Second, the stress view and the "sugar view" are used very little, even though these were the hardest to realise technically. Both Sven and Frida thought that these functions were the primary features driving sales for the company and the gap between actual use and expected use is perhaps the biggest surprise. It also concerns them as it may be a sign of people buying the bracelet because of the promise of these functions, but they then decide to stop using the bracelet as the functions do not provide the promised value.

The gap between actual use and expected use might often be a big surprise.

After an in-depth discussion, the two decide that they lack understanding of why the use of the views is so different from what they expected. Sven decides to interviewing several users and scanning product reviews and other sources of comments on their product. Frida feels that the data contains more information than what has been unveiled so far and decides to do some additional analysis trying to uncover more interesting usage patterns.

REFLECTION

Frida and Sven have just gone through a full iteration of the data loop. As is very typical when companies start to work with more data-driven approaches, a gap between the expectations and beliefs in the company and the actual drivers and behaviours of customers was uncovered. This often is uncomfortable as it forces the team to question everything they thought they knew about the customer, but at the same time, it is much better for a team to act on true customer insight and understanding than on shadow beliefs. A shadow belief is a belief widely held in an organisation or team that, however, is not supported by data and typically actively disproven. Shadow beliefs exist at an almost subconscious level and are very difficult to displace. Shadow beliefs are particularly toxic for customer-oriented companies as teams, based on these beliefs, act against actual customer needs while believing they are serving these needs.

A shadow belief is a belief widely held in an organisation or team that, however, is not supported by data and typically actively disproven.

ENTERING THE SECOND ITERATION

Frida and Sven have now completed a first, complete iteration of the human data loop. Based on the insights gained during the first loop, they are now entering the second loop. The first step in the loop is the collection of data. In this case, this only applies to Sven as Frida already has the data she needs to conduct her analysis. However, as the data collection from the QMB bracelets still runs, she decides to run her analysis on the entire data set, including the data that came in after her previous analysis.

Frida decides to look at how long each view is held before the user moves on to the next view. So, the analysis calculates the average time that a view is visible before it is replaced with the next view. In the Table 4, the results of the analysis are shown. Please note that the duration is now expanded with seconds as it was necessary to show the relevant information.

Table 4. Average time each view is visible.

View	Duration
TimeView	04:10:23
CalorieView	00:50:12
StressView	00:00:13
HeartRateView	00:56:54
SugarView	00:00:21

While Frida is analysing the quantitative data, Sven spends several hours interviewing users and looking at product reviews to better understand why users are using the bracelet in the way that is shown by the data. After talking to around ten users, a pattern starts to evolve and Sven uncovers a couple of relevant insights. As one can see in Table 4, especially the stress and sugar views are shown only very briefly. The reason, Sven learns, is that users consider the stress and sugar views as highly personal and do not want to share the data with others. They check these views only when others cannot see the screen of their bracelet and then move on to another view to make sure no sensitive data is visible. Second, users employ the calorie and heart rate views especially while exercising. The quantified self community is not only very focused on measuring all aspects of their existence, they're also health and exercise focused and work out on a very regular basis.

When Sven turns to the product reviews and customer feedback data that the company has available, the next realisation is that many users would like some form of stopwatch functionality to be added to the bracelet. Others want other functions like timers and alarms to be added. The reason many people request these features is because they use the bracelet as part of their workout routine, in their kitchen while cooking and they sleep wearing it. This means that users are making the device a part of their lives and habits to a point that few technologies accomplish. The key challenge is to continue developing the device and its software to a point where it is even better aligned with the needs of its users.

6 OPTIMIZING FEATURES

In the first chapter, we focused on using data to develop an insight into how our QMB bracelet was used in practice. Based on the data that we collected, we developed new insights that we can use to make changes to our product. The next step is to use data to optimise features so that these align better with the needs of customers.

The basic notion of optimising a feature is a four stage process. The first is to establish a baseline, i.e., the current performance of a feature. The next is to develop an alternative implementation of all or part of the feature and to deploy it to a subset of the user base while maintaining a control group. Subsequently, we collect data on the performance of the old version and the new version. Finally, we analyse the data from both groups of users in order to determine whether the alternative implementation worked or not.

THE OPEN LOOP PROBLEM

Product management is the function concerned with selecting the features and functionality to be included in a product release. Product managers tend to collect customer and user input in various ways, determine the relative priority of features and agree on a release content. The defined release content is given to R&D for building, testing and subsequent deployment.

Product managers, however, hardly ever return to earlier decisions concerning features with the intent of validating whether the expected value of each feature was indeed realised. As we know that many features are never used, it should be obvious that many decisions taken by product managers are wrong. We refer to this problem as the "open loop" problem. Product managers and owners do not get feedback on their decisions and consequently have no ways to adjust their decisions based on feedback from earlier decisions.

OPTIMISING QMB FEATURES

 Before starting to optimise features, one has to select a feature to optimise and have an idea on how to optimise the feature. After Sven and Frida discussed the data that they collected, they decided to focus on the stress view. Their data shows that the users are very interested in tracking their stress levels during the day, but don't want this to be clearly visible to others around them. Based on this insight, they sketch on a view that shows time and a small "red — yellow — green" indicator showing current stress level. This can be added as a sixth view on the bracelet. For users that would get the view added to their software, the mobile phone app will contain information on this and allow users to turn off the view.

Sven and Frida feel that there is enough potential interest from customers to warrant an experiment, but they are keen on not introducing the new view to all customers. Also, they want to make sure that the new view indeed leads to more use of the stress data collected by the bracelet. This, they realise, is the perfect setup for an A/B test (also referred to as split testing).

Depending on your definition, the notion of A/B/n testing originates in marketing or is the embodiment of the scientific method. The concept is concerned with a controlled experiment where a group of subjects is randomly assigned to alternative A or B (or any other available alternative). The experiment is intended to test a hypothesis which is defined as a relevant change in output or behaviour. The outcomes for each subject are recorded and, using statistical analysis, the test is intended to determine whether alternative A or B statistically leads to better outcomes, hence answering the hypothesis.

To realise the A/B test, Frida spends some time adding the sixth view to the QMB software and making its visibility optional depending on the settings on the server that allows the bracelet to determine whether to show the experimental view or not. After some internal testing, the software is ready for deployment.

SELECT USER BASE FOR EXPERIMENT

Once the technical setup for the experiment has been completed, the next discussion then becomes who to involve in the experiment. In most of the descriptions of A/B testing at Web 2.0 companies, it seems like every user is subject to experiments. However, in practice, companies need to be careful in allocating users to segments and using these segments for randomly assigning users in an experiment group and a control group. Especially when companies start to run multiple experiments, it requires that users are allocated only to multiple experiments if these are without question free from interference with each other.

The basic question, however, is the impact that the experiment will have on the perception and engagement of users. One can experiment with wildly different implementations of part of the product functionality, but this can easily lead to a backlash by users who feel they're used as guinea pigs by the company rather than it  focusing on delivering value for its customers. As the customers of QuaMe are very passionate users of the QMB bracelet and, by extension, very passionate about quantifying themselves, they have little patience for things that interfere with their primary reason for using the product. As Sven and Frida are just starting with experimentation and A/B testing, they decide to play it safe. During the initial development of the bracelet, they had a group of passionate users (Friends of QuaMe - or FQM) that were willing to test out the device. They decide to start with using that group for the experiment.

The first approach that Frida and Sven consider is to assign FQM as the experiment group and the rest of the users as the control group. However, they are concerned that the FQM users will behave different from the other users and that this will skew the results of the experiment. Based on this analysis, Frida and Sven change their approach and decide to only use FQM users for the A/B test, meaning that both the experiment group and the control group are taken from the FQM community.

Frida runs a script on the FQM database to randomly assign the members to the experiment group and the control group. Frida has written the QMB software in such a way that the sixth view (showing time and a graphical indicator of stress levels) is only visible if the device ID is present in a server-side database. That allows her to release the software to all users, even those that are not in the FQM community, as their device IDs will never be in the database. Also, the sixth view has its own event ID (#1106), so the events can still be put in the regular events database for future analysis.

ESTABLISH BASELINE

So far, Frida and Sven have figured out everything by themselves, but as they are concerned with the quality of the decisions they will be taking on the data, they decide that some expert help might be useful. Luckily, Sven knows a statistician from the time he was a student and he knows she lives in the same city. So, he reaches out to Alva and she agrees to come by after work to share her perspective. After Frida and Sven explained what they've done so far and what they plan to do next, Alva is duly impressed but has one recommendation that requires the team to adjust their plans a little bit.

The original idea that Frida and Sven had was to use the data that they collected in the first round as a baseline and compare the experiment data to the control group and the historical data. Alva, however, recommends that they run a baselining phase. During the baselining, the control group and the experiment group both get the new software, but the "B" version (the sixth view) is turned off. Although this is conceptually not necessary as one should be able to collect the same data from the control group while running the experiment, Alva points out that there have been many cases where a small, simple mistake in the setup caused companies to make decisions that were wrong and that hurt the company. Alva convinced the team that establishing a baseline is a small insurance premium that they would pay to avoid this and that the cost of taking a wrong decision is much higher than the cost of the insurance premium.

Based on the input from Alva, Frida makes a small adjustment in the code to allow the experiment to be turned on and off (which, in hindsight, is a good idea to have in general) and runs the test suite to ensure that things are working as they should, that the experiment can be turned on and off and that the data is collected as intended. Once she is satisfied, she triggers the deployment of the software, causing the bracelets out in the field to update their software with the latest version.

At this point, Sven and Frida need to decide how much time to take for establishing the baseline. If they were statistics experts, they could have done all kinds of smart stuff, but Alva is out on a trip for the coming two weeks, so they devise a formula where they calculate the difference between the relative view length for both groups and convert this to a percentage.

As an example, after the first day, the control group has used the time view for 17:37 and the experiment group has used it for 18:47 minutes. The difference is 70 minutes. Converting this to a percentage is done by calculating the average time for both groups (18:12) and then dividing the 70 minutes by the average time. This becomes $70/((18*60)+12) = 0.0641$ or 6.41%. By repeating this for each view and averaging the percentages, they get a percentage indicating the difference between the two groups. As they use all data collected since the start of the experiment, they expect the difference to approach 0% when the experiment is structured correctly. If they have made a mistake, the difference will converge on another number.

In the Table 5 , Sven and Frida summarised the difference calculation after each day. Even though the difference starts out higher than what Sven and Frida expected, they notice that each day the difference roughly halves. After 6 days, the difference has hit 0.5%, which is what they had defined as their boundary for having established a successful baseline. Based on this, they decide to turn on the experiment.

Table 5. Successful baseline – difference is approaching 0%.

Day	Difference between the experiment group and the control group
1	12,30%
2	6,50%
3	3,10%
4	1,80%
5	0,80%
6	0,50%

RUNNING THE A/B EXPERIMENT

Sven and Frida have activated the experiment, which means not only that the bracelet will show a 6th view to the experiment group, but also that the mobile app contains information about the new view that is only shown to the experiment group. They have carefully worded the information page to indicate that the time+stress view is under development, but avoided to indicate to FQM community that they are part of an experiment. Although some members may guess as much, we're looking to influence the experiment as little as possible.

As the data starts to come in, however, Frida realises that they haven't been sufficiently precise in defining what would constitute success for the experiment. She asks for some time from Sven and the two of them sit down to hash things out. The main reason for entering this experiment was that the QMB bracelet has some pretty advanced capabilities, such as measuring stress, that distinguish it from competing products. However, if users do not use these advanced capabilities, the differentiation and pricing power that QuaMe has will erode over time. Hence, Sven and Frida are looking for ways to make people use all the features of QMB. So, the main question for the experiment is: does providing a limited presentation of stress levels on the time view increase use of the stress tracking functionality?

The main question for the A/B test leads to two more detailed questions that can actually be derived from the data. First, is the time+stress view preferred over the time view when both are available to a user? Second, does the use of a time+stress view result in increased use of the stress view in the system? The latter then broken down into two more detailed questions. First, is the stress view used more in the experiment group than in the control group? And, second, are users that prefer the time+stress view over the time view more likely to use the stress view?

As the FQM community is about 1000 people strong, it means that around 500 people get access to the new time+stress view. The QuaMe team could have chosen another division than 50/50, but they decided to keep things as simple as possible. Because of the relatively limited depth of the points, the team decides to run the experiment for at least two weeks and to continue running it until the numbers have become sufficiently stable (again, they're aiming for about 0.5%).

Rather than running the experiment and then analysing the data afterwards, Frida builds a solution that analyses the data daily and she presents the data on the main dashboard screen as one of the rotating views. As one can see in Figure 1, it is clear that users rapidly adopt the time+stress view over the original time view. It is also clear that the time+stress view is the preferred view of around 85% of the users that have access to it while there is a group of 15% that still uses the time view. Of course, the control group, only having access to the time view, still uses that view for 100%.

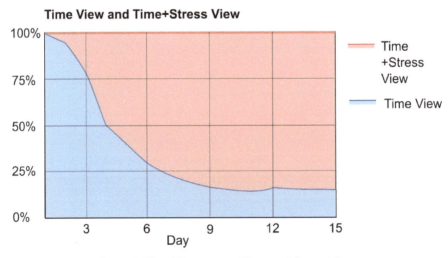

Figure 1. Time View versus Time and Stress View.

The next question the team was interested in was the relative use of the stress view for users of the time+stress view versus users that only use the time view. The expectation was that the increased awareness of the stress view would lead to higher use by the time+stress view users. However, after analysing the data (see Table 6) this expectation was not met at all. In fact, users that have access to the time+stress view hardly use the stress view at all. This data is completely unexpected by the team and requires them to quite fundamentally adjust their view of the user behaviour. After combining the qualitative user feedback with the data, the conclusion that Sven and Frida reach is that users care about a high-level view of their stress levels but have no need for a detailed view on their bracelet.

Table 6. Relative use of views for different groups.

View	Time+Stress	Time Only	Control
Time	79,70%	75,90%	76,70%
Calories	13,10%	15,20%	14,90%
Stress	0,10%	0,50%	0,40%
Heart rate	6,60%	8,10%	7,60%
Sugar	0,50%	0,30%	0,30%

GENERALISING THE EXPERIMENT

When selecting the user base for the experiment, the team selected their Friends of QuaMe community as the group to conduct the experiment on. As these users are the most positive towards the company, this clearly is a strategy to reduce risk as the likelihood of permanently damaging the relationship with these users is significantly lower than when working

with the entire user community. At the same time, however, there is a risk that the behaviour of the FQM users is not representative for the community at large. To avoid this risk, one of the potential strategies is to repeat the experiment in a broader scope with the intent of confirming the findings.

Frida and Sven discuss this risk and decide to repeat the experiment with the entire user base. As they seek to just confirm the findings from their experiment with the FQM community, they decide to run this experiment with a much smaller experiment group percentage of 3%. This means that 97% of the user base will act as control group whereas a randomly selected 3% is exposed to the time+stress view. Although this means the experiment will need to run longer to collect sufficient data, this is again a mechanism to reduce risk as only a few users are exposed to the new view.

Similar to the FQM experiment group, Frida first runs a baseline stage to confirm that everything is running as it should. Once she is satisfied, she turns on the experiment and shows the daily results on the company dashboard. As shown in Figure 2, the adoption pattern by the general user base is a bit slower than by the FQM users, but overall follows the same pattern. With this, the team confirms that the FQM users and the overall user base are behaving largely similar.

FQM and overall user base

Figure 2. Adoption of Time+Stress view by FQM and general user.

SIMPLIFYING THE PRODUCT

The results from the experiment involving the entire user population leads Frida and Sven to consider whether the time view should be removed altogether. At the same time, there are suggestions by users that suggest that the time+stress view is not the only view that users would want. Some users want to use the indicator to show sugar or heart rate levels. Based on this, the team decides to replace the time view as well as the time+stress view with a configurable time+ view where the user, through the mobile companion app, can configure the indicator on the time+ view to use the indicator for several different options. The additional advantage is that only the user of the bracelet now knows what lightweight indicator on the screen means, which further increases the privacy of the view. Of course, in line with earlier work, the team instruments the software with data collection functionality in order to track the adoption by users. In parallel, it keeps an eye on feedback from customers through social media and customer support, but there are few negative responses and the positive ones by far outweigh those.

REFLECTION

Frida and Sven have completed the first significant change in their bracelet that was fully driven and validated by data. During the process, we learned that it is very easy to have opinions and beliefs that are extremely convincing in discussions, but that turn out to be completely wrong when the data is collected. For any organisation, it is critically important to frequently validate beliefs that are often widely held in the organisation as the market might change and the organisation may take decisions that are not optimal due to incorrect, shadow beliefs.

For any organisation, it is critically important to frequently validate (shadow) beliefs that are often widely held in the organization.

7 VALUE MODELLING

Early in the life of QuaMe, Sven and Frida realised that whatever wearable product they were going to have, a mobile app to accompany it would be critical to its success. At that point, they were stretched thin with just designing and delivering the QMB bracelet and consequently they decide to outsource the app development to a team in Asia. That was certainly the right decision at the time, but as QuaMe is developing as a company and generating revenue, Sven and Frida have also been able to hire some strong people around them.

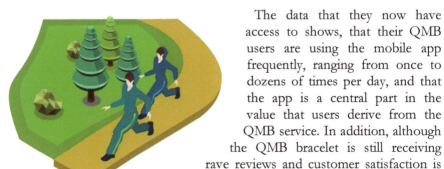

The data that they now have access to shows, that their QMB users are using the mobile app frequently, ranging from once to dozens of times per day, and that the app is a central part in the value that users derive from the QMB service. In addition, although the QMB bracelet is still receiving rave reviews and customer satisfaction is high, the feedback on the mobile app is much more mixed and the "suggestions" box on the QuaMe website predominantly receives suggestions for improvements to the mobile app.

The team decides that the time has come to bring development of the mobile app in house and decides to hire a pair similar to themselves. This means a product manager/user experience person and a developer with deep understanding of all the relevant mobile operating systems as well as data analytics skills. Using their network and social media, they find several really promising candidates and after a time consuming interview process, they manage to hire Nils as a mobile app developer and Ebba as a mobile UX expert and product manager. Both Ebba and Nils have mostly worked in e-commerce contexts where the mobile app is predominantly a support for the main website. The e-commerce domain, however, is extremely data-driven and both have extensive experience with various types of mobile analytics tools.

SYSTEMATIC VALUE MODELLING PROCESS

In collaboration with several companies we have developed a systematic value modelling process for modelling and tracking feature value during development. The process provides detailed guidance on how to quantify feature value in such a way that it can be systematically validated over time. We outline the process in the steps below and then provide more in-depth illustration of the steps using the QuaMe case study later in the section.

1 Identify key value factors

Key value factors are what the feature is intended to improve and for which metrics are implemented so that they can be tracked over time. The key value factors are defined for top-level, sub-level and team-level goals.

2 Agree on intended direction of the key value factors

When the key value factors have been identified, the next step is to decide what is good and what is bad, i.e. if a factor should go up or down as a result of the experiment. As part of any experiment, the key value factors will move either up or down, i.e. increase or decrease in value. Therefore, and in order to know whether an experiment is successful or not, there needs to be a common agreement on the direction each key value factor should move in. This helps understanding what constitutes customer value and in what direction the factors need to move to reflect improved value to customers.

3 Normalisation of the key value factors

To get an accurate result of an experiment, the key value factors need to be normalised so that they operate on a comparable scale. For example, while value factors such as 'new users' and 'recurrent users' have similar ranges, a factor such as 'revenue' will have a very different range and cannot be easily compared. To cater for this, each key value factor needs to have an upper and a lower boundary and a mapping function to map the result to a value between 0-1.

4 Prioritisation of the key value factors

The next step is to determine the relative importance of each factor. As experiments will likely influence some factors positively and some negatively, we need to be able to decide which alternative in an A/B test is the preferred one. The value function will typically include several key value factors that are all important to optimise for. However, as these might not be equally important, teams need to prioritise the relative weight, i.e. importance, of these factors. This prioritisation between factors will help understand what constitutes a successful experiment. The prioritisation is expressed in the value function by assigning the relative weight to each value factor, e.g. 0.2*new users + 0.3*recurring users + ... etc. It is typically easiest to have the sum of the weights equal to 1.

5 Translation of hypothesis into an experiment

When the key value factors are defined, normalised and prioritised, the hypothesis can be converted into an executable experiment. The hypothesis represents an idea, i.e. an invalidated assumption about what adds value to customers, and is picked from the feature backlog in which potential new features are described.

6 Selection of a system or user base for experimentation

Once the hypothesis is translated into an executable experiment the appropriate base of deployed systems or active users is selected. If the experiment, and the key value factors, relate solely to product operation and performance, a system or sub-system is selected. However, if the experiment is directed towards improving or optimising customer-oriented functionality a suitable user segment needs to be identified. The selected base is subsequently divided into an experiment group and a control group.

7 Establishing baseline

The baseline is set before the experiment is initiated and it represents the values of the key factors without any interference with the system. Typically, this is done by providing the control group and the experiment group with the same base solution ('A') in order to verify that there is no statistical difference between these groups and that they get the same outcome when exposed to the new software (the 'B' version is turned off to ensure that both groups try the same solution before initiating the A/B experiment).

8 Establishing length of experiment

Different experiments require different timeframes. Typically, and in order to capture both weekdays and weekends, they run at least 7 days. Some experiments run for 2-3 weeks to make sure that a change is not only a novelty effect but something with impact over time. Some queries require seasonal experiments to reflect changes in behaviours. However, too long experiments should be avoided as they cause users or systems to enter, leave and re-enter the experiment. This makes the experiment more difficult to control and it makes the result less trustworthy.

Too long experiments should be avoided. It makes the experiment more difficult to control and further - the result less trustworthy.

9 Initiate experiment

When initiating the experiment, the control group gets the base solution 'A' (as established as the baseline) and the experiment group gets the "treatment" solution 'B' of the software. During the experiment, user or system behaviours are measured to decide which version of the software that has the most positive impact on the key value factors and that help optimise towards the agreed upon value function. While the experiment is running there are two activities that need to be conducted. Activity 1 is to constantly verify the guardrail metrics (as described in step 3 above). Activity 2 is to constantly verify statistical validity of the data between the experiment and the control group.

10 Completion of experiment

There are three possible results of an experiment. Either, there is statistical validity of the data and the experiment can be concluded. In this case, the base solution ('A') or new solution ('B') is implemented for all users or systems going forward. Alternatively, no statistical validity is achieved before the end of the experiment. In this case, the experiment is concluded and the base solution ('A') is implemented for all users since no difference could be identified between the two. Finally, if the experiment causes systems to get outside their guardrails, the experiment is aborted.

It should be noted that for any experiment there are four types of outcomes. There are the *expected positive factors* and the *expected negative factors*. In addition, and as a potential surprise to most companies, there are the *unexpected positive factors* and the *unexpected negative factors*. Also, as the whole notion of experimentation and testing hypotheses is an iterative process, additional factors might have to be added to the value function during an experiment and due to increasing insights about these four types of factors. For example, if a team realises that what they optimise for, and the outcome of such an experiment, proves to harm overall sales this needs to be adjusted by adding or removing factors.

The approach we present strives to increase the awareness of experiments as part of a larger business context. In this context, value modelling on all levels of the business is critical in order to avoid sub-optimisation that will harm the company in the long run. In our future research, we aim to address

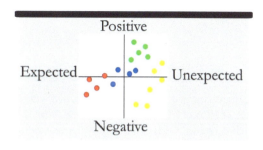

this further by exploring how the value function is part of a larger business context in which knowledge evolve as the result of both qualitative and quantitative customer and product data.

FEATURE BACKLOG IN THE QUAME MOBILE APP

As Ebba and Nils come on board, the first thing they do is to review all the feedback that QuaMe has received concerning the mobile app. The second action they take is to review all the feedback on the QMB bracelet to identify items that could be addressed by the mobile app. The result is an impressive list of over 50 feature requests that they have to consider. When analysing the features, they notice that there are several categories of features that these features can be put into. In Table 7 we show some examples of the categories and the features in each category.

Similar to virtually any software-intensive systems company in the world, the number of features that the Ebba and Nils could build for the mobile app far exceeds their ability to build actual features. This means that they need to be very selective in what they prioritize and decide to build.

Table 7. Overview of feature category and feature examples.

Feature category	Example feature
Time-based views	Compare today's heart rate to the same day last week
Alternative uses of data	Analyze my sleep using the motion sensor data
Social	Show my friend's workout next to mine
Configure QMB	Rotate periodically through predefined set of views

THE USER BEHAVIOUR GAP

One of the hardest learnings is to understand that what people say they want or do is not the same as what people will actually do when put in the situation that they were asked about. There are numerous examples of this available and everyone with even a modicum of self awareness will have realised this about themselves. The typical example is the New Year's commitment that many people make about going to the gym three times per week after the first of January. Even if you do go a couple of times, the vast majority of people soon loses the habit and falls back in earlier behaviour. Another example is security versus convenience. When asked, mobile bank app users will almost always prioritise security over convenience in using the mobile app. However, practice shows that a secure banking app that is inconvenient to log into is not used, despite the requests from customers. And, vice versa, a less secure but convenient app is used all the time, despite potential security risks.

What people say they want or do is not the same as what people will actually do.

The key takeaway is that we can use what customers and users say as a starting point, but that we always need to confirm what they told us with research into their actual behaviour. In fact, whenever the option presents itself, one should always choose user behaviour over other input as the basis for decisions. As we have discussed earlier, the best way to study user behaviour is to run experiments in deployed software and to measure the relevant aspects of customer or system behaviour.

PRIORITISING FEATURES AT QUAME

Nils and Ebba have now collected a large number of features that they could potentially build to improve the mobile app. As they can't build everything and the throughput of new features will be relatively low, as they are only two people, they need to find ways to focus their energy on the most important features that provide the most value for the company and its customers. The traditional way to do this is to rely on the product manager and perhaps some selected customers for the prioritisation. Based on the input from customers, the product manager will then prioritise the features and put them in the feature backlog in the desired order.

Although Ebba has worked with the traditional way of feature prioritisation in the past, she has learned the hard way that the prioritisation that she has made in the past have frequently turned out very different in terms of customer value than what she expected beforehand. This could of course mean that Ebba just isn't a very good product manager, but she has seen many other cases where product managers were very excited about certain features or products and were singing the praises of the expected outcomes. When the feature or product was actually built, the reality proved to be quite different.

However, no one likes to be confronted with a mismatch between what they expected and the actual outcome. In addition, product managers often work predominantly in the front end of the process. This means that by the time a feature or product is released, the product manager will already be working on something else. This results in what we call the "open loop" problem: product managers prioritise features and products based on their best understanding of the priorities and expect certain outcomes. However, they seldom verify whether the expected outcome is actually realised. As a consequence, there is no feedback loop that allows product managers to develop better intuitions and to learn about their prioritisation. Hence, we're not getting better.

MODELLING FEATURE VALUE

The "open loop" problem that we discussed in the previous section can be addressed by creating a better definition of what the expected value of a feature actually constitutes and then tracking the realisation of this feature value over the development process. The first step for this is to model the value of the feature in a fashion that we can actually measure this. To measure the value of a feature, we need to express it in terms of factors that can be collected from the deployed system in an automated fashion. This does not have to mean that we only need to rely on factors that are already collected as we can instrument the system with additional functionality to collect data.

Earlier in the book, we discussed the notion of instrumentation. We did not discuss, to the same extent, the sometimes tenuous connection between what we really would like to measure about the customer or the system and the factors that can be easily connected from deployed systems. As William Bruce Cameron so eloquently said: "Not everything that can be counted counts. Not everything that counts can be counted."

Model the value of the feature in a fashion that you can actually measure it.

As Ebba has experienced that the 'guestimation' approach in product management is not working terribly well, she is committed to working in a different way with features. However, she first needs a prioritised list of features. So, after Ebba and Nils have collected the features they have been able to discern from all the sources they had available, the whole team decides to spend a couple of hours sorting through all the features and prioritising these as a single, prioritised feature backlog. However, different from traditional, agile work practices where the backlog is the interface between product management representing the customer and the R&D organisation, the team agrees that this backlog only represents their best understanding of what will likely add value to customers. They also decide that they get data from the development of the first features, they will reevaluate the backlog. Their ambition is to make this a periodic process where once every couple of months they review all their learnings and agree on re-prioritisation and course corrections.

"Not everything that can be counted counts. Not everything that counts can be counted."
~ William Bruce Cameron

One result of the feature backlog creation workshop is that the team decides to prioritise social features. Their assessment is that focusing on social features, especially around the unique data collected by the bracelet, will likely increase customer satisfaction and drive sales of QMB. One of the features that the team identified is to compare results when working out together with a friend and the agreement is to start with this feature for extending the mobile app.

Based on this prioritisation, Ebba and Nils sit down to identify the key factors that they'd like to measure. As a main, top-level factor, they agree that customer satisfaction should be the key focus and that the feature should result in an improvement of customer satisfaction. Although there are many ways to measure customer satisfaction, QuaMe has so far focused on the Net Promoter Score (NPS) and they agree the NPS of users of the feature should be 5% higher than that of users that do not use the feature.

The challenge with NPS, of course, is that it tends to move relatively slowly and that it is influenced by many aspects. Consequently, it is harder to influence by a single feature and it may take a long time before the metric starts to move in response to the feature having been introduced. The danger of relying too much on a performance indicator that is hard to influence is that all your efforts to improve the system may fall flat because the impact, at least in the short term, fall below the statistical relevance boundary and consequently get lost in the noise.

In response to analysing their ability to influence the NPS score, Ebba and Nils realise that they need indicators that are more closely linked to the feature itself and more directly influenced by changes that they make to the mobile app. The simplest thing to measure is the frequency of use and the funnel associated with it. When focusing on frequency of use, the first question one can ask is: what percentage of users that are made aware of the feature use it at least once? The real value creator is of course the building of a habit around the feature and this requires repeat use. So, Ebba and Nils decide to also measure whether users still use the feature after 1, 2, 4, 8 and 12 weeks. Although many Web 2.0 companies focus on daily active users (DAU) and monthly active users (MAU), Ebba and Nils decide to focus on the funnel of repeat use and to track when they lose users in the habit building process. Finally, the team decides that it would be better if a user would use social features with more friends rather than with fewer friends, so they not only measure, over time, the frequency of use, but also the number of social network connections with whom they have used the social functionality. In Figure 3, the factors and the relationships between the factors are shown. As illustrated in the figure, frequency of use is only one of the factors influencing the net promoter score. The figure does not show the time delay between higher level and lower level factors, but this is an important aspect in tracking of feature value.

As Ebba and Nils have now modelled the factors influencing frequency of use, they look to formulate a value function that captures the relative importance of different factors. As the model that they developed is quite complex concerning repeat use, they decide to initially only focus on repeat use during the first week. The factors selected for the value function are three:

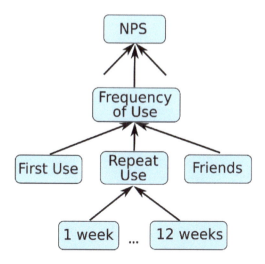

Figure 3. Part of the value factor network population.

- **First use:** This factor measures the percentage of users that uses the collaborative training feature at least once after having been exposed to it. The direction of the feature is "up", meaning that a higher number is a better result. The factor does not need to be normalised as it already is a percentage and consequently between 0 and 1.

- **Repeat use:** The repeat use factor measures the percentage of first use users that have used the feature again after a week. Similar to the first use factor, higher is better and the factor, being a percentage, is already normalised.

- **Friends:** The final factor is the percentage of a user's friends that he or she decides to invite for collaborative training. Again, a higher percentage is better.

Based on that, the value function becomes the following:

$$Vf = X * \% \text{ First Use} + Y * \% \text{ Repeat Use (1 week)} + Z * \% \text{ Friends}$$

The way to read the function is that it consists of three factors, i.e., first use, repeat use and number of friends. First use is the percentage of users that, after being exposed to the feature, will use it at least once. Repeat use is concerned with the percentage of users that use the feature at least one more time within the week after they used it for the first time. Finally, the percentage of friends represents the relative share of friends that the user invites for collaborative workouts. The mobile app already allows for a selection of one's Facebook friends to be added to the mobile app, so QuaMe knows for each user how many friends each user has added to the mobile app.

Although value functions can be modelled in many different ways, it is preferable if we can model it such that it indicates a range between a theoretical minimum and a theoretical maximum. For instance, our value function follows this principle. If all users that are exposed to the feature decide to adopt it and every user uses it again within a week and invites all his or her friends, the feature has reached the maximum value it can theoretically achieve. Similarly, if nobody uses the feature and invites no friends, the feature provides no value. Although this value function does not allow for negative value to be created, there are situations where some factors contribute negatively to created value and if there are no factors generating positive value, the overall value function may turn out negative.

Our value function contains three constants, X, Y and Z. The intent of these constants is to provide the relative importance of each of the factors. Again, for simplicity reasons, we set as a constraint that X + Y + Z = 1. That means that each of the constants can be between 0 and 1 (again, we're ignoring the negative value for now) and the sum should be 1. After extensive discussions, Ebba and Nils decide to prioritise first use, giving X a value of 0.5, and de-prioritise friends, giving Z a value of 0.2, which leaves 0.3 for Y. The resulting value function is now:

$$Vf = 0.5 * \% \ First \ Use + 0.3 * \% \ Repeat \ Use \ (1 \ week) + 0.2 * \% \ Friends$$

Based on our selection of constant values, our value function can now generate an outcome between 0 and 1. After reviewing this with Frida and Sven, Ebba and Nils agree to use this as a basis for tracking progress while introducing the collaborative training feature.

ESTABLISHING CUSTOMER INTEREST

Although Ebba and Nils worked hard on modelling the feature value and there is a significant amount of indication that users want to train collaboratively, Ebba still feels that they may be acting too much on wishful thinking. So, before starting the development of the feature, she agrees with Nils to run a pre-development experiment before committing to developing the first version of the feature. The mobile app that they have just taken over has the ability to show a popup message in the startup screen. So, when the user starts the app, the first thing that can happen is a popup. The popup is intended to inform users of updates to the app, but Ebba and Nils decide to hijack the popup for informing users of the collaborative training feature. The popup will have a button that says "Learn more" and the goal of the experiment is to understand how many users will actually want to learn more. Although this is only an indication of customer interest, it provides more data than the current information available.

After Nils finishes the code associated with the "Learn more" button and the popup has been configured, they decide to release it but expose only a small percentage of users (initially 1%) to the popup. Once the data starts to come in, it becomes clear that around a third of the users click on the "learn more" button, which is a sufficiently strong interest for Ebba and Nils to confirm the relevance of the feature. As the "learn more" button also recorded the identity of the users that clicked on it, the team now also has a group of potentially interested users that they can use to start testing early versions of the feature with.

BREAKING DOWN FEATURES

Ebba and Nils decide to build the feature in an iterative fashion and to collect data after each iteration. The intent is to use the data to deciding if more should be added to the feature and, if so, what the next part of the feature is that should be built. The collaborative training feature has at least four aspects to it:

- **Same time; same place:** Two or more bracelet users train together, e.g., a joined run, and can compare their statistics, such as heart rate, after the run.

- **Same time; different place:** Two (or more) users can both decide to go for a workout at the same time, but are in different places. For instance, both users can go for a 10K run and compare their statistics, including speed and heart rate, after the run.

- **Different time: same place:** Some friends can do the same workout, e.g., running a specific 10K route, but at different times and compare their statistics.

- **Different time; different place**: Remote friends can agree on a similar workout and compare statistics afterwards.

Once the basic aspect of the collaborative training feature are in place, there are still several ways to extend it. The initial focus will be on outdoor, aerobic exercises such as running and biking. However, one could focus on other types of workouts, such as weight training, as well. Also, Ebba and Nils focus on the mobile app and as such are more concerned with comparing workouts after they took place as not everyone is interested in carrying their mobile phone while working out. However, one could imagine that extending the functionality to the bracelet would be an option. In this case, the bracelet would inform its user of his or her performance in relation to the person or persons training with or comparing to.

The above break down of features can virtually always be performed for a feature. When studying the characteristics of a feature in more detail, it quickly becomes clear that the feature that is discussed actually consists of several smaller chunks of functionality that can be built without having to build everything else at the same time. As we aim to build our products using data, we would like to build the feature iteratively and measure during the process how customers use the feature and then adjust accordingly.

INTRODUCING HYPEX

The process of feature development described in the previous section is a model that we have formalised in HYPEX. HYPEX is an abbreviation of "Hypothesis - Experiment" and describes a process for iterative feature development combined with the value modelling that we have done so far. As shown in Figure 4, the process starts with a feature backlog and the selection of a feature out of the backlog. The step after that is to determine what the expected behaviour of the feature is. This means: what will be the measurable aspects of system behaviour or customer behaviour that will change in response to this feature being added. Obviously, these measurable aspects are the same elements as those used in the value modelling that we discussed earlier.

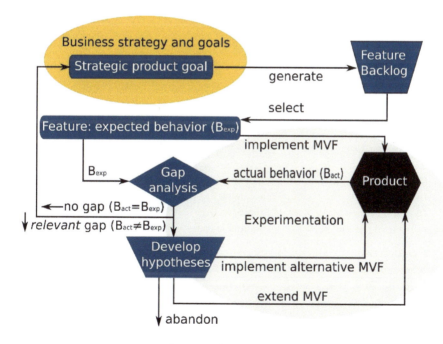

Figure 4. The HYPEX model.

Once we have agreed what we expect and what the business justification for building this feature is, the next step is to build the first slice of the feature. The prioritisation should be done such that the slice of the feature selected to build first should also be expected to give the largest contribution to the expected behaviour and, consequently, to the value function. This first slice, we refer to as the minimal viable feature or MVF. As necessary, we do not only build the feature but also add the necessary instrumentation to the system software to ensure that we can measure the actual behaviour of users or the system itself. Once the MVF and necessary instrumentation have been built, this version of the software can be deployed to systems in the field.

Once the software is deployed, we will start to get the data back from the systems in the field and this data will allow us to determine the actual behaviour of users or of systems. Once we have statistically relevant data from the field, we can compare the actual behaviour to the expected behaviour and in virtually all cases, there will be a gap between the two. This gap is then analysed by the team in order to take one of four actions:

- **Abandon**: If there is no shift at all in actual behaviour after the MVF is added to the system, it is clear that the hypothesis proved to be incorrect. At this point, it's best to drop the feature from the system and move on to the next feature in the backlog.

- **Finish**: If the gap between expected and actual behaviour is very small, the team can decide to declare the feature finished, even though significant parts of the feature have not been implemented yet. However, there really is no point in continuing if the goal has already been reached.

- **Expand**: If there is a relevant shift in the actual behaviour, but not enough to close the gap sufficiently, the team can proceed to build the next slice of the feature in order to try to further close the gap between expected and actual behaviour.

- **Re-implement**: The final alternative is concerned with the team realising that the way they realised the MVF was at odds with the way users want to use the feature or the way the system actually behaves in practice. This then can result in a decision to scrap the existing MVF implementation and to re-implement it based on the new insights.

The process, of course, continues to iterate through feature expansion or reimplementation until the gap is sufficiently small or until the team decides that the feature does not deliver on its promises and should be abandoned. Depending on the feature, the experience and knowledge of the team and type of system, the HYPEX process may move through a few or several iterations before returning to the backlog to select the next feature.

The HYPEX model conveniently does not discuss the notion of concurrency in development. As most R&D organisations have multiple R&D teams, there will typically be multiple instances of the HYPEX process ongoing. In addition, the data collection stage of HYPEX to establish actual behaviour is not instantaneous and often requires a significant amount of time, e.g., weeks. In that case, even a single R&D team will be working on multiple features in parallel as they wait for the data collection for one feature to complete.

Finally, as multiple experiments will be ongoing at the same time, the statistical analysis of the data becomes more complicated as these experiments may influence each other, requiring a certain level of vigilance when analysing the data. However, applying some intelligence to the sequencing of experiments and avoiding concurrent running of experiments affecting the same value function factors and selection of user groups for each experiment allows for a pragmatic realisation of this approach to development.

MEASURING ACTUAL FEATURE VALUE

Returning to Ebba and Nils and the collaborative training feature they are looking to build, they discussed the different aspects of the feature and decided that the "same time; same place" slice of the feature will likely contribute the most to the value function. As the value function that we introduced earlier has three factors (first use, repeat use and number of friends), these factors will need to be collected by the system if we are to establish the actual value of the feature. As the collaborative training feature requires the server for the storing of friends and training data, the instrumentation can mostly be done in the server code, even though some part still takes place in the software on mobile device. This simplifies the process significantly.

As Nils builds the software for the minimal viable feature (MVF) and the instrumentation on the server and in the mobile app, Ebba spends her time figuring out the target group to address in the first release of this feature. It turns out that they have the identities of a couple of hundred users that have expressed interest in the feature and many of those are active in running or cycling. Out of this group, the majority has added their friends to the mobile app as well. Ebba decides to randomly select 100 users that (1) have shown interest, (2) engage in running or cycling and (3) that have at least two friends in their QuaMe friends network. When Nils finalises development and testing, they release the feature to the selected users and inform them through the popup in the mobile app that the feature is now available for use.

They decide to collect data for two weeks before drawing any conclusions. The reason for this is that many people have a weekly training schedule so it can take up to one week for a collaborative training opportunity to appear and in order to measure repeat use, they need to wait at least another week before the data around the repeat use becomes available. After two weeks, however, the numbers are in and the team gathers to review the results.

As shown in Table 8, 70% of the users that were selected for the trial decided to use the feature at least once. This is a great result, but not entirely representative of all users of the QMB bracelet as the group that was selected had already indicated interest in the feature.

Table 8. The first round of collaborative training feature development.

Collaborative Training Feature	First iteration
First use	70%
Repeat use	30%
Friends	5%

The second data point is that 30% of users decided to use the feature again in the first week after having used it for the first time. Again, this is a promising result especially considering the fact that we have only built a small part of the feature. The final data point shows that users only invited 5% of their friends on average. This is a really confounding data point as many QMB users do not have that many friends in the QMB mobile app and 5% means that only some users invited some of their friends to the collaborative training feature. The team decides to investigate this further. In the meantime, however, the value function for the feature after the first iteration is:

$$Vf = 0.5 * 0.7 + 0.3 * 0.3 + 0.2 * 0.05 = 0.45 \text{ or } 45\%$$

The team considers this a very good outcome as the first iteration of the feature realisation has already reached close to half of the theoretically maximum value.

REVISING THE VALUE FUNCTION

When iterating through the HYPEX process, the value function will have to be reconsidered for every iteration. The reason is that we will likely see four types of outcomes. As shown in Table 9, the experiment will have factors that contribute to the feature value as well as factors that withdraw from the value. Also, there will be factors that we expected to be influenced by the feature and there are features that we did not expect to be influenced.

The unexpected factors require us to revise the value function after each iteration as the implications of a feature may extend significantly beyond the originally modelled factors.

SECOND ITERATION: SOLVING THE FRIENDS PROBLEM

The team was surprised at the low use of the friends function and a bit disappointed as the reason for starting with collaborative features was to increase the social stickiness of the QMB bracelet. Ebba and Nils agreed to investigate the rationale for the low usage and they decided to simply reach out to the users in the feature experiment group to get qualitative input on the feature. After some dozen calls, it becomes clear that the main reason for the low use of the friends part of the feature is that users use the friends feature primarily for contacts they don't meet often in real life. For their friends that they meet at the gym or running club, they don't have connections in the mobile app as they so far have not felt the need to do so.

Table 9. Four categories of feature experiment factors.

Feature Experiment Outcomes	Expected	Unexpected
Positive	These factors are the *reason we build the feature in the first place* as these contribute to the value function and justify the building of the feature.	Once the data of a feature experiment comes in, we may identify additional factors that we did not expect to be influenced but that contribute positively to the value of the feature.
Negative	When adding functionality, there may be factors that are detrimental. This is acceptable as long as the positive factors outweigh the negative ones.	Similarly, the feature experiment may uncover unexpected factors that negatively affect the value of the feature.

Once the team realised this, they decided to extend the functionality of the feature with a one-button-click adding of contacts when two QMB users are in the same location. In addition, they decided to revise the value function account for the new insight:

$$Vf = 0.3 * \% \text{ First Use} + 0.3 * \% \text{ Repeat Use (1 week)} + 0.1 * \% \text{ Friends} + 0.3 * \% \text{ Local Friends Added}$$

The new value function adds a new factor, providing an indication of the percentage of other QMB users that a user meets that get added as training friends. As the bracelet and the mobile app continuously track location, the company can determine, by analysing the data, when QMB users are in the same location simultaneously. By analysing the historical data from the first experiment, Ebba and Nils are able to estimate that of the friends added, most are local, so they estimate the new factor to be around 4%. In addition, the new value function lowers the importance of first use and of connecting with existing friends for training and stresses the local friends that get added.

When expressing the value of the value function after the first iteration using the new formula:

$$Vf = 0.3 * 0.7 + 0.3 * 0.3 + 0.1 * 0.05 + 0.3 * 0.04 = 0.317 \text{ or } 32\%$$

After Nils wrote the code for the one-click adding of local friends and even added a pop up in the mobile app suggestion to connect with someone who happens to be in the vicinity, the team deploys the new code to the same user base and decides to again collect data for two weeks. At the end of the period the data comes in and the result is as shown in Table 10.

Table 10. Result after the second iteration.

Collaborative Training Feature	Second iteration
First use	75%
Repeat use	40%
Friends	5%
Local friends	17%

Using the value function, we get the following score:

$$Vf = 0.3 * 0.75 + 0.3 * 0.4 + 0.1 * 0.05 + 0.3 * 0.17 = 0.401 \text{ or } 40\%$$

Although the feature still has a long way to go to reach its theoretical maximum, the last iteration is a significant improvement over the last version of the feature.

8 CONCLUSION

Humans and organisations easily develop habits that define their behaviours and that cause them operate based on opinions and patterns formed during earlier experiences. In a world that is evolving increasingly fast, there is a significant risk of taking decisions that go against the best interests of customers and the company itself. The best way to address this risk is by adopting data-driven and evidence-based practices where decisions are taken based on data instead of based on opinions, habits and behavioural patterns. This approach is of course centuries old and is commonly referred to as the scientific method.

In data-driven and evidence-based practices decisions are taken based on data - instead of opinions, habits and behavioural patterns.

With the increasing ability to collect and analyse vast amounts of data and the relentless drive towards lower cost of storage and computing due to Moore's Law, organisations have unprecedented means to adopt data- and evidence-based decision making in areas where we earlier were not able to do so. One of these areas is the development of software-intensive systems.

As software-intensive systems are becoming increasingly connected, many companies have adopted continuous deployment of new software for systems deployed in the field. Although developing the capability to do this in a reliable, consistent fashion without major quality issues is a challenge in and of itself and, it is not the focus of this short book. We focus on the capability to communicate with deployed products as this provides unprecedented capabilities to collect data  from these products. This data can be used to learn about customer behaviour, product performance as well as the outcome of experimentation conducted on these products.

In this short book we explored the basics of exploiting the data collection capability. We studied the use of features in the product and the implications of making changes to the product software. Also, we started to explore the notion of value modelling as a mechanism to ensure the delivery of proven value to customers and for the company.

9 FURTHER READING

Rather than putting lots of references in the text, I wanted to share some of the books and papers that I have been involved in and that form the basis for this short book.

1.   E Backlund, M Bolle, M Tichy, HH Olsson, J Bosch, Automated user interaction analysis for workflow-based web portals, International Conference of Software Business (ICSOB 2014), pp. 148-162, 2014.

2.   J Bosch, Speed, Data, and Ecosystems: The Future of Software Engineering, IEEE Software 33 (1), pp. 82-88, 2016

3.   J Bosch, Speed, Data and Ecosystems: Excelling in a Software-Driven World, CRC Press, ISBN 9781138198180, 2016.

4.   P Bosch-Sijtsema, J Bosch, User Involvement throughout the Innovation Process in High-Tech Industries Journal of Product Innovation Management 32 (5), pp. 793-807, 2015.

5.   A Fabijan, HH Olsson, J Bosch, Time to Say'Good Bye': Feature Lifecycle, 42th Euromicro Conference on Software Engineering and Advanced Applications (SEAA), pp. 9-16, 2016.

6.   A Fabijan, HH Olsson, J Bosch, The Lack of Sharing of Customer Data in Large Software Organizations: Challenges and Implications, International Conference on Agile Software Development (XP 2016), pp. 39-52, 2016.

7.   A Fabijan, HH Olsson, J Bosch, Early value argumentation and prediction: an iterative approach to quantifying feature value, International Conference on Product-Focused Software Process Improvement, pp. 16-23, 2015.

8.   A Fabijan, HH Olsson, J Bosch, Customer feedback and data collection techniques in software R&D: a literature review, International Conference of Software Business (ICSOB 2015), pp. 139-153, 2015.

9.   HH Olsson, J Bosch, Towards continuous customer validation: a conceptual model for combining qualitative customer feedback with quantitative customer observation, International Conference of Software Business (ICSOB 2015, pp. 154-166, 2015.

10.   H Olsson, A Sandberg, J Bosch, H Alahyari, Scale and responsiveness in large-scale software development, IEEE Software 31 (5), pp. 87-93, 2014.

11.   HH Olsson, J Bosch, From Opinions to Data-Driven Software R&D: A Multi-case Study on How to Close the 'Open Loop' Problem, 40th EUROMICRO Conference on Software Engineering and Advanced Applications (SEAA 2014), pp. 9-16, 2014.

12.   HH Olsson, H Alahyari, J Bosch, Climbing the" Stairway to Heaven"--A Multiple-Case Study Exploring Barriers in the Transition from Agile Development towards Continuous Deployment of Software, 38th Euromicro Conference on Software Engineering and Advanced Applications (SEAA 2012), pp. 392-399, 2012.

ABOUT THE AUTHOR

Jan Bosch is professor of software engineering at Chalmers University Technology in Gothenburg, Sweden. He is director of the Software Center (*www.software-center.se*), a strategic partner-funded collaboration between 10 large European companies (including Ericsson, Volvo Cars, Volvo Trucks, Saab Defense, Jeppesen (Boeing) and Siemens) and five universities focused on software engineering excellence.

Earlier, he worked as Vice President Engineering Process at Intuit Inc where he also led Intuit's Open Innovation efforts and headed the central mobile technologies team. Before Intuit, he was head of the Software and Application Technologies Laboratory at Nokia Research Center, Finland.

Prior to joining Nokia, he headed the software engineering research group at the University of Groningen, The Netherlands. He received a MSc degree from the University of Twente, The Netherlands, and a PhD degree from Lund University, Sweden.

His research activities include evidence-based development, software architecture, innovation experiment systems, compositional software engineering, software ecosystems, software product families and software variability management. He is the author of several books including "Design and Use of Software Architectures: Adopting and Evolving a Product Line Approach" published by Pearson Education (Addison-Wesley & ACM Press) and "Speed, Data and Ecosystems: Excelling in a Software-Driven World" published by Taylor and Francis, editor of several books and volumes and author of a significant number of research articles. He is editor for Journal of Systems and Software as well as Science of Computer Programming, chaired several conferences as general and program chair, served on numerous program committees and organized countless workshops.

In the startup space, Jan is chairman of the board of Fidesmo in Stockholm, Auqtus and, until recently, Remente, in Gothenburg, Sweden. He serves on the advisory board of Assia Inc. in Redwood City, CA, Peltarion AB in Stockholm and Burt AB in Gothenburg, Sweden.

Jan also runs a boutique consulting firm, Boschonian AB, that offers its clients support around the implications of digitalization including the management of R&D and innovation. For more information see his website: *www.janbosch.com*.